INDEX

US Secret War in Africa..

Armed Islamic Group- GIA...

Salafist Group for Preaching and Combat (GSPC)...............

Al-Qaeda in the Islamic Maghreb (AQIM)........................

Al Murabitoun..

Jund Al Khilafa...

Ansar Dini..

US Secret War in Africa

One night in November 2003, beneath the moon-washed waters off Somalia's northern coast, a small, dark shadow slipped away from the attack submarine Dallas and headed toward the shore.

The smaller shape was a 21-foot-long submersible called a SEAL delivery vehicle. Launched from a tubular dry deck shelter on the sub and designed to infiltrate Navy SEALS on covert or clandestine missions, the SDV carries its crew and passengers exposed to the water, breathing from their scuba gear or the vehicle's compressed air supply. Aboard were a handful of SEALs on a top-secret special reconnaissance mission into a country with which the U.S. was technically not at war.

The SEALs grounded the SDV on the ocean bottom and pushed away from it, taking with them the centerpiece of their mission, a specially disguised high-tech camera called a Cardinal device.

Unbeknownst to them, during the previous 24 hours, their mission had been the subject of Cabinet-level debate in Washington and had almost been canceled until President George W. Bush gave the go-ahead.

Now they were conducting what a special operations source with firsthand knowledge of the operation referred to as "a long swim through some of the most shark-infested waters in the world" toward the coastline that loomed ominously ahead of them. The hard part was just beginning.

The classified mission was an early volley in a decade long effort to hunt down al-Qaida operatives in the Horn of Africa. Waged largely out of sight by U.S. special operations forces and the CIA, the campaign has featured hard-fought and dramatic successes, extraordinary risk-taking and a lot of frustration.

If there was a moment that launched the campaign, it came in January 2002 in a frigid electrical closet at Afghanistan's Bagram Air Base. FBI Special Agent Russ Fincher and New York Police Detective Marty Mahon were interrogating Ali Abdul Aziz al-Fakhri, a Libyan known by his nom de guerre, Ibn al-Shaykh al-Libi.

One of the most important prisoners taken up to that point in the war, al-Libi had run al-Qaida's Khalden training camp, which counted "shoe bomber" Richard Reid and Zacarias Moussaoui, the convicted 20th hijacker of the Sept. 11 plot, among its hundreds of graduates.

Using classic interrogation techniques, Fincher and Mahon built a relationship of trust with al-Libi such that the captive talked volubly, giving up much valuable intelligence. What has not previously been reported is what al-Libi told Fincher and Mahon about al-Qaida's plans to regroup if and when the terrorist organization were forced from its safe haven in Afghanistan. According to a military source who was in Bagram during the Afghan war's early months, al-Libi laid out al-Qaida's "multiphased approach."

The first phase was to flee to Pakistan's tribal areas that abut Afghanistan "but be prepared because of the way things were going to go further." The bottom line of al-Qaida's plan, the military source said, was: *We need to reconstitute and the next sanctuaries in which to do that are Yemen and Somalia.*

The mission

The SEALs conducting the clandestine camera missions were part of a secret task force established just for that operation. Its commander, Special Forces Col. Rod Turner, also headed two other elements that shared forces and had overlapping chains of command.

One was Joint Special Operations Task Force-Horn of Africa, which fell under Combined Joint Task Force-Horn of Africa in Camp Lemonier, Djibouti. The composition of CJTF-HOA has shifted significantly over the years, but by far its largest operational component in 2003, the task force's first full year of existence, was Turner's 350-400 person joint special operations task force.

With the exception of its small staff, the JSOTF doubled as U.S. Central Command's crisis response element, or CRE, a force led by Turner and available to the CJTF-HOA commander for direct action, special reconnaissance and personnel recovery missions, but which also could be tasked for other missions by CENTCOM commander Army Gen. John Abizaid.

The CRE was a robust force package. It included:

• A Special Forces commander's in-extremis force, or CIF, company. A CIF is highly trained in direct action and available to conduct no-notice high-risk missions for the geographic combatant commander its parent SF group supports.

• A SEAL platoon, which usually includes two officers and 14 enlisted.

• A Naval Special Warfare rigid-hull inflatable boat, or RHIB, detachment.

• An Air Force special operations package that included four MH-53 Pave Low helicopters and two MC-130P Combat Shadow fixed-wing turboprop aircraft, designed to conduct low-visibility or clandestine air-to-air refueling and infiltration missions, as well as about 200 personnel.

The entire CRE, plus another contingent of SEALs equipped with the SEAL delivery vehicles, also belonged to a third task force commanded by Turner that he stood up for a single highly classified operation that came down from Defense Secretary Donald Rumsfeld

It was that operation that found the SEALs swimming toward the Somali shore on the first of about a dozen missions to install the Cardinal devices along the Somali coastline.

The cameras were disguised to look like natural or other man-made objects, so as not to arouse suspicion. The aim was to place them facing locations such as potential al-Qaida training camps or piers where al-Qaida personnel were suspected of arriving.

The devices were set to photograph the locations and then transmit the images automatically via satellite back to what a senior intelligence official described as "a limited pool of customers" in the U.S. The targets along the northern coast were code-named Cobalt Blue while those along the eastern coast were code-named Poison Scepter, said the special operations source with firsthand knowledge of the operation.

With its combination of derring-do and high-tech gadgetry straight out of a James Bond movie, the mission was by no means universally popular among the few U.S. officials who had prior notice of it. The U.S. ambassador to Kenya, William Bellamy, and the CIA station chief in Nairobi, Kenya, John Bennett, were opposed to the whole enterprise. Because Somalia had no effective government, and therefore no U.S. Embassy, the CIA ran its Somalia campaign out of Kenya.

The plan was to emplace 17 cameras along the Somali coastline, according to the special ops source. But the embassy "didn't see the wisdom in any of them," said an intelligence source with long experience in the Horn. In Bellamy's view, the hidden camera operation "was overkill,".

The question being asked in the embassy was, "*Why are we creating this Ferrari when all you had to do was pay a guy to go in*" and set up the cameras. To U.S. officials in Nairobi, it appeared to be the SEALs who were pushing hard for the mission.

Matters came to a head 24 hours before the first Cobalt Blue mission was due to launch. Bellamy called the CJTF-HOA commander, Marine Brig. Gen. Mastin Robeson, and asked him to stop the mission because it would put agency assets in danger. Robeson, one of only four people in the CJTF-HOA headquarters who knew about the missions, refused because the operation was being conducted at the direction of the defense secretary. But Bellamy repeated his request in a cable to Robeson.

Within hours, the argument had reached Rumsfeld and Director of Central Intelligence George Tenet. The two senior officials argued their respective cases to the president, who quickly came to a decision: Execute the Cobalt Blue targets as planned and renegotiate the others with the embassy. As a result, of the 17 cameras, "we ended up putting 12 to 14 in," the special ops source said.

Dangerous waters

The SEALs preparing to execute the first Cobalt Blue mission knew nothing about this back and forth, and power politics did not affect the mission timeline. That first target's identity remains classified, but it was chosen because it was the least challenging of the northern set of missions.

For the Cobalt Blue missions, a single Navy flattop was positioned off the coast, courtesy of 5th Fleet. The flattop functioned as the command ship for Cmdr. Mark Mullins, who was in charge of the SEALs conducting the SDV missions, according to the special ops source.

Air Force special operations AC-130 Spectre gunships based in Kuwait provided air cover for the Cobalt Blue targets. But the gunships didn't have the range to support the Poison Scepter missions, so for the eastern leg of the operation, 5th Fleet provided a second flattop with Marine Corps AH-1W Super Cobra attack helicopters aboard to provide close-air support, if needed.

"Fifth Fleet was very helpful in providing assets at different periods for different lengths of time that they put under [our] command and control to be able to conduct classified operations" said a senior CJTF-HOA official from the period, who declined to talk about the SEAL missions in detail.

The flattops stayed 60 to 70 miles out at sea during the day, but the one that functioned as Mullins' command ship and which also carried the RHIB element would come closer on nights the SEALs were going ashore.

The AC-130s and Super Cobras were not the only backup available to the SEAL elements. There were also two separate quick-reaction forces available for each mission. One was another SEAL element in RHIBs floating near Mullins' command ship that could race in if the SDV team got into trouble near the shoreline. The other consisted of a couple of 12-man Special Forces operational detachments-alpha, or A-teams, drawn from A Company, 1st Battalion, 5th Special Forces Group.

Between the gunships, the SEALs bobbing up and down in their RHIBs and the SF soldiers waiting with Navy HH-60 helicopters.Once the SEALs had swum ashore, their first task was to find the right spot to emplace the camera. Although the general locations had been selected ahead of time, the SEALs "had to make the final site selection themselves," said the special ops source.

This required a combination of tactical skill and raw courage, given that they were often operating in urban and semi-urban terrain. They did some ballsy stuff — these things were not stuck out in the middle of nowhere. The SEALs were operating in some of the most heavily congested areas in Somalia.

For about 24 hours prior to the mission, overhead coverage of the target location came courtesy of Navy P-3 Orion reconnaissance planes flying from the Seychelles augmented by the Dallas' periscope.

Stealthy shooting

The SEALs used photos taken by the P-3 to help decide where to put the cameras.But the SEALs also had the flexibility to change their decisions once they had come ashore. The cameras' ingenious design gave them numerous options.

On at least one occasion, the best place for the camera turned out to be on a rusted, wrecked ship in a harbor. On another occasion, the SEALs put the camera on a breaker made of rocks near a pier.

The farthest the SEALs had to travel upon hitting the beach was "less than a mile," but they had to move stealthily while carrying "pretty heavy equipment. After emplacing the Cardinal device, the SEALs had to test its ability to take and transmit a photo before they returned to the Dallas.

On most of the missions, which stretched over a six-week period in November and December 2003, the SEALs spent about 2½ to three hours ashore, but one mission required them to spend five to six hours out of the water.

It was critical that the SEALs were not seen at any point during the mission. With targets located in or near major ports like Kismayo and Merka in southeastern Somalia, this presented a major challenge. But the SEALs stayed undetected and made it back safely from each mission.

Armed Islamic Group- GIA

The Armed Islamic Group, known by its French acronym, Armed Islamic Group, waged a violent war against Algeria's secular military regime during the 1990s. Though terrorism continues to plague Algerian society, the GIA's role in current violence appears to have abated. The GIA grew out of a 1992 decision by Algeria's military government to cancel an election in which it appeared that a moderate, mainstream Muslim party, the Islamic Salvation Front (FIS), was headed for victory.

The backlash took many forms, including formation of the Islamic Salvation Army, a militant group linked with the FIS. But the separate and more radical GIA soon gained a notorious reputation for mayhem and murder, targeting those affiliated-even remotely-with the military and the government, as well as innocents and foreign nationals. The GIA vowed to raze the secular Algerian government and, in its place, establish a Muslim state ruled by sharia, or Islamic law.

The ensuing civil war ranked as one of the most violent in the world during the 1990s but petered out in 2002 following a cease-fire declared by the Islamic Salvation Army, a group that never condoned the civilian violence perpetrated by the GIA. In its most active period in the 1990s the GIA established a presence in France, Belgium, Britain, and Italy. While the GIA is now largely defunct, it remains designated as a foreign terrorist organization by the U.S. State Department. Algerian and Western counterterrorism officials say that many members may have defected in recent years and joined al-Qaeda or its sister organization al-Qaeda in the Islamic Maghreb (AQIM).

One of the GIA's leaders, Antar Zouabri, has proclaimed: "*in our war, there is no neutrality. Except for those who are with us, all others are* renegades." International press during the 1990s focused on the large number of journalists and intellectuals who were beheaded or whose throats were slit during Algeria's civil war. GIA leaders were quoted as saying, "*those who fight against us by the pen will die by the sword.*" Journalists were considered to be supporters of the military regime and a secular society. The GIA had enormous animosity toward the media, and particularly Algerians who wrote in French, the language of the former colonial power.

The extremist Islamic background of the GIA also included a disdain for liberated women. Women not wearing the hijab, or headscarf, women in professional careers, or women who refused mu'ta, the practice of temporary marriages of pleasure, were often murdered. The GIA was especially known for—and received much criticism for—killing the female relatives and children of the military. The group justified this by citing an extremist concept called takfir, which is a form of excommunication. In these cases, takfir was used to label a Muslim associated with the military regime as an infidel and therefore game for attack.

The group also expressed a vehement opposition to the presence of foreigners in Algeria. During the civil conflict, over 120 foreign nationals were killed by the GIA. France, which supported the military government, became a target as well. The GIA orchestrated international terrorist attacks in the country, most notably the 1994 hijacking of an Air France plane and the bombing of two Paris Metro stations the following year. Other Western countries were also accused of meddling in Algerian affairs; in 1995 the GIA issued a threatening communiqué demanding that all Western embassies and foreigners leave the country.

Jews, Christians, and even moderate Muslims were also among the GIA's targets. Al Ansar, or The Supporters, a weekly GIA newspaper with headquarters in Europe, frequently published inflammatory rhetoric against Jews and Christians. Several Muslims who professed their wish to use diplomacy with the government were killed and their deaths publicized to set an example. The wantonness with which the GIA killed Muslims contributed significantly to its demise.

Like lots of violent Islamic movements around the world, many militants in the GIA appear to trace their radicalization to Afghanistan, where they fought as mujahadeen, or Islamic guerillas, against the Soviet army from 1979 to 1989. As Afghan returnees, these radicals sought to transplant the idea that secular government is, by definition, illegitimate and repeat their success in Afghanistan against the Algerian regime.

Other GIA members included advocates of violent political change who were disenchanted with the moderate FIS's reliance on rigged political processes. But as a group, the GIA only became coherent in 1992 when the military preempted the FIS electoral victory. Many members of the FIS were arrested and several paramilitary groups formed in response to the government's crackdown. The GIA emerged as one of several radical FIS splinter factions and quickly became the dominant terrorist organization in the country. By 1994, it was recruiting upwards of five hundred young men a week into its ranks.

The U.S. State Department dates the GIA's last significant terrorist attack to 2001, but this is debated. Some sources attribute the group with unclaimed terrorist attacks up until 2005, though the Salafist Group for Preaching and Combat (GSPC) is the more likely culprit. The Salafists, who ultimately became Al Qaeda in the Islamic Maghreb, eclipsed the GIA in numbers and popularity in 1998 by denouncing indiscriminant violence against civilians - a trademark of the GIA.

The Salafists subsequently subsumed most of the GIA's networks and financial resources in Europe. The final blows came in 2004, when Algerian police forces launched a widespread crackdown on all local terrorist groups. Over four hundred members of both the GIA and the Salafists were arrested in that sweep.

Sayyed Imam Al-Sharif, one of the chief ideologues of the global jihad movement, writes that leaders of al-Qaeda extolled the GIA's actions to further popularize global jihad. Ayman al-Zawahiri, a prominent al-Qaeda leader, even provided religious justification for the GIA's violent tactics. On the other hand, some experts say that al-Qaeda leader Osama bin Laden distanced himself and al-Qaeda from the GIA and instead supported the more popular GSPC, further contributing to the GIA's decline.

The armed groups rose to prominence after the military intervened in the political process in early 1992. It declared a state of emergency, deposed President Bendjedid, outlawed the FIS and imprisoned its leaders, and detained thousands of Islamic activists in Saharan concentration camps. In October 1992 leaders of armed Islamist factions convened a meeting at Tamesguida, attempting to form a united front.

But after a surprise raid by security forces aborted the meeting, suspicions of infltration by DRS double agents prevented any such unity. The GIA formed in late 1992 as a loose umbrella group of certain disparate Islamist movements fighting the Algerian military. Sidestepping the FIS, it soon took the lead in what became a jihad to establish an Islamic state. The GIA represented a challenge to the FIS's leadership of the Islamist movement as much as it did opposition to the government. Radical "Afghans," such as Qari Said, were partly responsible for the polarization between the FIS and the GIA.

The GIA commenced its campaign of terror in early 1993, attacking military posts, but also non-military targets, including foreigners, intellectuals, and journalists. By late 1993 the FIS regretted conceding leadership to the intransigent, extremist GIA. In July 1994 the more moderate FIS formed the Armée islamique du salut (AIS, Islamic Salvation Army) as an armed alternative to the GIA.

The AIS, in its public statements, allowed for the possibility of a return to the electoral process, while the GIA did not. In October 1994 Djamel Zitouni became national amir of the GIA. Zitouni concentrated more on the power struggle with the AIS than on opposition to the government.

In January 1996 the GIA publicly declared war on the AIS, labeling them apostates also. At the same time that civil war raged between the military junta and the Islamists, another civil war was being fought between the GIA and the AIS. Later that year the radical Antar Zouabri became national amir of the GIA. Zouabri blamed the civilian populace for not supporting the jihad. The death toll in the conflict soared as GIA fighters concentrated their attacks on "collaborating" civilians.

Zouabri issued a fatwa titled *"The Great Demarcation"* labeling the entire Algerian people kufr (impious) for failing to support its campaign against "le Pouvoir," the government. This hard-line policy cost the GIA both international credibility and domestic support. Prominent Arab jihadi groups, including Ayman al-Zawahiri's Egyptian Islamic Jihad (EIJ) and the Libyan Islamic Fighting Group (LIFG), broke publicly with the GIA over their excessive resort to takfir. The bloodiest year of the Algerian civil war saw over forty separate massacres of civilians, most attributed to the GIA.

Salafist Group
for Preaching and Combat (GSPC)

It was in this milieu that the GSPC emerged, growing out of elements of the GIA leadership, including Hassan Hattab, Shaykh Abou al-Baraa, and Saïd El-Para. These dissidents rejected the GIA's policy of attacking civilians, allowing only military targets. Hattab broke with the GIA in late 1996 because of the group's excesses. The AIS, also disgusted with the GIA's brutality, declared a unilateral cease-fire with the government in October 1997, thus setting the stage for later government offers of amnesty. The GSPC formed in 1998, vowing to concentrate attacks on security forces, not civilians.

Hattab became the new group's leader, al-Baraa its ideologue, and Saïd a field commander. Al-Qa'ida and bin Laden, having repudiated the GIA's anti-civilian attacks, gave their blessing to the GSPC. By 2000, though still adhering to the GIA goal of an Islamic state in Algeria, the GSPC had also verbally embraced Al-Qa'ida's ideology of global jihad.

By 2002 the GSPC claimed to have over 4,000 fighters and was concentrating its attacks on Algerian military convoys and bases. In September 2002 Bouteflika ordered a crackdown on the GSPC, Algeria's largest anti-Islamist operation in five years. The Group responded with stepped-up raids, including an attack led by Saïf on a convoy near Batna in January 2003 that killed forty-three soldiers.

Despite the GSPC's new global rhetoric, Hattab remained committed to national jihad, but his leadership was challenged by rival amirs who had a more internationalist outlook, including Nabil Sahraoui, Abdelmalek Droukdel (a.k.a. Abu Musab Abdelwadoud), and Saïf. Saïf's kidnapping of thirty-two European tourists in the Tassili Massif was a challenge to Hattab.

In September 2003 Hattab was deposed as GSPC leader for the more radical Sahraoui. Saïf, meanwhile, along with Belmokhtar, was extending GSPC operations to Algeria's Sahelian neighbors.

In a global context, the GSPC's most threatening aspects were its reported links with Al-Qa'ida and the expansion of its activities beyond Algeria to Europe and to the Sahelian countries. At the time of the GSPC split, Al-Qa'ida was seeking to disassociate itself from the GIA and welcomed the GSPC because of its pledge not to attack civilians.

Amar Makhlulif (a.k.a. Haydar Abu Doha), a London-based Algerian trained in Qa'ida camps in Afghanistan, had been one of the first to urge Hattab to split from the GIA. Abu Doha helped reorganize the GIA's former European networks under Qa'ida aegis with GSPC control.

US intelligence estimates suggested that there may have been as many as 800 GSPC operatives in Europe in 2006. By that time the GSPC had claimed responsibility for numerous terrorist actions involving the Sahelian countries, especially Mauritania and Mali, and was deeply implicated in regional smuggling and trafficking activities.

After the GSPC officially merged with al-Qa'ida (AQ) in September 2006 the organization became known as al-Qa'ida in the Islamic Maghreb (AQIM). On February 20, 2008, the Department of State amended the GSPC designation to reflect the change and made AQIM the official name for the organization. Some senior members of AQIM are former Armed Islamic Group (GIA) insurgents.

On March 11, 2004 news sources reported that a firefight had occurred between the Chad military and an Algerian terrorist group, Salafist Group for Preaching and Combat (GSPC). This firefight, which is believed to have resulted in the death of some 43 GSPC members, apparently began in Niger and crossed into Chad. The fighting took place over two days. The group, led by a former Algerian soldier named Saifi Ammari and nicknamed "the Para," had been tracked across the Sahara from its bases in the Algeria-Mali border area. It is not clear if "the Para" was involved in the attack.

Little known outside Algeria, the GSPC burst onto the international scene in early 2003 with the spectacular kidnapping of thirty-two European tourists
in Algeria's southern desert massifs. The kidnapping was resolved after the German government reportedly ransomed the hostages. But the perpetrators, led by a mysterious GSPC amir (leader) named Amari Saïf (a.k.a. Abdelrezak El-Para), were tracked down in a dramatic four-country chase across the desert, culminating in the capture of Saïf in northern Chad.

This joint action, reportedly given logistical support by US forces of the European Command (Eucom), was generally credited to the new Pan Sahel Initiative (PSI), the first organ of the US program of securitization of the Sahel, which involved Mauritania, Mali, Niger, and Chad. Though groundwork for the PSI had begun before the kidnapping, Saif's daring action and the GSPC itself quickly became the principal justifications for the American initiative. Congress subsequently expanded the PSI into the Trans-Saharan Counter-Terrorism Partnership (TSCTP), involving nine North and West African countries, including Algeria, America's new African partner in the War on Terror.

The US and Algeria forged ahead with their securitization programs in the Sahel despite concerns that a US military presence in the region would make the security situation there worse, not better, and allegations that Saïf might have been abetted by elements of the Département du Renseignement et de la Sécurité (DRS, Department of Intelligence and Security), Algeria's military intelligence agency. Meanwhile, the GSPC, under another mysterious desert amir, Mokhtar Belmokhtar, appeared to be moving in the direction of "hybrid" terrorist organizations, as concerned with contraband trafficking as with anti-government resistance.

By early 2007 the GSPC had morphed once again into AQIM, an Al-Qa'ida affiliate pledging loyalty to Osama bin Laden's global jihad. It will be argued that changes in the posture of the GSPC/AQIM suggest that the organization is more concerned with its own survival than with either of its previously stated goals: overthrowing the Algerian government or advancing global jihad. It will also be argued that the US and Algeria have made use of and perhaps exaggerated the threat posed by GSPC/AQIM to justify their own goals: for the Americans, a military and economic foothold in Africa; for Algeria, the continued rule of its authoritarian government.

Al-Qaeda in the Islamic Maghreb (AQIM)

Al-Qaeda in the Islamic Maghreb (AQIM) is a Salafi-jihadist militant group and U.S.-designated foreign terrorist organization (FTO) operating in the Sahara and Sahel. The group traces its provenance to Algeria's civil war in the 1990s and has in the past decade become an al-Qaeda affiliate with regional ambitions.

AQIM and its offshoots pose the primary transnational terror threat in North and West Africa but are unlikely to strike in the United States and Europe, according to U.S. officials. The flow of militants from the Sahara and Sahel to Syria and Iraq, where thousands of Moroccan and Tunisian citizens have joined terrorist groups, is raising concerns about battle-hardened fighters returning to these relatively stable countries.

Background

AQIM's lineage extends back to a guerilla Islamist movement known as the Armed Islamic Group (GIA), which violently opposed Algiers' secular leadership in the 1990s. The insurrection began after Algeria's French-backed military canceled a second round of parliamentary elections in 1992 when it appeared that the Islamic Salvation Front was poised to win power.

In 1998, several GIA commanders grew concerned that brutal tactics, such as beheadings, were alienating their Algerian constituency and broke away to found the Salafist Group for Preaching and Combat (GSPC). GIA, now defunct, was delisted as an FTO in 2010.

GSPC initially drew popular support by vowing to continue the rebellion without killing civilians, but a government amnesty and counterterrorism campaign drove it into disarray in the early 2000s.

Baya to AQ

The group aligned with al-Qaeda in the 2000s to stage high-profile attacks and improve recruiting and fundraising. Ayman al-Zawahiri, al-Qaeda's leader, who was at the time second in command, announced the union on September 11, 2006, and GSPC rebranded itself as AQIM the following January.

The new name denoted the group's broadened aspirations, which after the merger included Western interests in addition to Algerian targets. Adopting the famous name may have enhanced AQIM's legitimacy among extremists and facilitated recruitment, while enabling al-Qaeda to burnish its international credentials and, potentially, access a region geographically close to Europe.

That year, 2007, marked the height of AQIM suicide attacks and other violent incidents in Algeria. In Algiers in December, AQIM simultaneously bombed the regional UN headquarters and the Algerian Constitutional Court, killing thirty-three people.

Strategy

AQIM's objectives include ridding North Africa of Western influence; overthrowing governments deemed apostate, including those of Algeria, Libya, Mali, Mauritania, Morocco, and Tunisia; and installing fundamentalist regimes based on sharia. AQIM's ideology blends global Salafi-jihadist dogma with regionally resonant elements, including references to the early Islamic conquest of the Maghreb and the Iberian Peninsula.

While these states of the Maghreb and Sahel are AQIM's "near enemy," the group has declared Spain and France its foremost "far enemies." France, in particular, has a long history as the region's colonial heavyweight, and its government continues to provide political and military support to local regimes AQIM opposes. AQIM leaders regularly threaten to stage attacks in France, and praised the Charlie Hebdo massacre in Paris in January 2015.

Network

The group has about one thousand members in Algeria and smaller numbers in the Sahel region, which includes areas in Chad, Mali, and Mauritania. It also has cells in Libya, Nigeria, and Tunisia. The group claimed responsibility for killing four policemen outside the home of Tunisia's interior minister in May 2014. It isn't clear if AQIM or affiliated fighters were involved in the attack on tourists in Tunis in March 2015 or the killing of Egyptian Christian hostages in Libya earlier that year. Groups professing links to the Islamic State claimed responsibility for both of those attacks.

AQIM has not attacked Europe or the United States, although individuals suspected to have ties to the group have been arrested in Germany, Italy, the

Netherlands, Portugal, and the UK. The UN Security Council's al-Qaeda sanctions committee says European cells are a source of the group's funding.

In 2012 AQIM had coordinated with other terrorist groups in the region, including Nigeria's Boko Haram, Somalia's al-Shabab, and Yemen's AQAP, with arms and funds flowing among them. Former Secretary of State Hillary Clinton and the former head of Africa Command, General Carter Ham, are among senior U.S. officials who said there were "links" between AQIM and the Libyan militants who attacked the U.S. diplomatic mission in Benghazi in September 2012, but these allegations have not been substantiated in subsequent reporting or unclassified investigations.

Much of AQIM's leadership is believed to have trained with other Arab volunteers—among them, Osama bin Laden—in Afghanistan during the 1979–1989 war against the Soviet occupation. Many returned to the Middle East and North Africa radicalized.

Structure

The group is divided into katibas, or brigades, which are organized in often-independent cells. AQIM's top commanders may be rivals as much as comrades or they may operate relatively autonomously. Chairman of the Joint Chiefs of Staff General Martin E. Dempsey likewise characterized AQIM as *"a syndicate of groups who come together episodically, when it's convenient to them, in order to advance their cause. Sometimes their cause is terrorism. Sometimes it's criminal. Sometimes it's arms trafficking."*

Algerian-born *Abdelmalek Droukdel* has led the group since 2004. Also known as Abou Mossab Abdelwadoud, he is a trained engineer and explosives expert. AQIM declared France its primary target under Droukdel's leadership. He was sentenced to death, in absentia, along with twenty-four other alleged terrorists, by an Algerian court in February 2015.

Mokhtar Belmokhtar, a founding member of AQIM who led a battalion on the Algeria-Mali border, broke with the group in late 2012 and created his own organization known as the al-Mulathamun Battalion (aka Those Who Sign in Blood Battalion). The one-eyed veteran of the anti-Soviet Afghan insurgency is believed to have masterminded the January 2013 hostage crisis at a natural-gas facility in eastern Algeria that left at least thirty-eight civilians dead, as well as twin suicide bombings in Niger that killed at least twenty-six in May of that year.

Operations

AQIM's tactics include guerilla-style raids, assassinations, and suicide bombings of military, government, and civilian targets. Its members have frequently kidnapped, and sometimes executed, aid workers, tourists, diplomats, and employees of multinational corporations.

The group raises money through kidnapping for ransom and trafficking arms, vehicles, cigarettes, and persons. AQIM's operational area saw an influx of arms in the aftermath of NATO's 2011 Libya air campaign.

Kidnappings not only raise funds, but also facilitate prisoner exchanges and discourage foreign enterprise in the region. In October 2012, David Cohen, Undersecretary for Terrorism and Financial Intelligence at the U.S. Treasury Department, said KFR was "the most significant terrorist financing threat today."

Belmokhtar's "family connections with local tribes allow [AQIM and affiliated groups] to capitalize on criminal opportunities in the southern Maghreb, such as smuggling, to finance terrorism," according to the UN sanctions committee. Cigarettes, a lucrative contraband, earned Belmokhtar the moniker "Mr. Marlboro."

AQIM also smuggles narcotics, providing a vital Sahel way station between suppliers in Latin America and European markets.

Partners in Mali

AQIM and splinter groups Ansar al-Dine and the Movement for Unity and Jihad in West Africa (MUJAO) aided the semi-nomadic Tuaregs—a historically disenfranchised regional ethnic minority—to launch a rebellion in early 2012 against Mali's government and wrest control of the country's sparsely populated North. They soon marginalized Tuareg forces and began implementing their own severe brand of sharia in the breakaway northern territory, implementing policies that were particularly brutal for women, according to the United Nations.

Mali, a predominantly Muslim, landlocked West African nation that straddles the arid latitudes of the sub-Saharan Sahel, gained independence from France in 1960. Its democratization over the past two decades had been celebrated by Western donor states, but the military coup in 2012 and ongoing Islamist insurgency have exposed deep and destabilizing political rifts.

After a brief union combating state forces, Ansar al-Dine and MUJAO drove Tuareg separatists out of major towns including Gao, Kidal, and Timbuktu. MUJAO merged with Belmokhtar's al-Mulathamun Battalion in May 2013 to form al-Murabitoun.

In December 2012, the UN Security Council authorized a military peacekeeping mission in Mali, known as MINUSMA, for which regional coalition Economic Community of West African States pledged thousands of troops. However, a rebel advance southward in January 2013, prior to the deployment of African forces, prompted Bamako to request immediate military assistance from France. French forces retook Gao, Kidal, and Timbuktu, pushing AQIM militants northward into the mountains.

Militant Islamists have retreated from major towns, though they have sporadically attacked MINUSMA troops. At least twenty-two peacekeepers have been killed since September 2014, according to a January 2015 UN Security Council report, highlighting the insecurity that remains in the country's North.

The African-led peacekeeping mission never reached full operational capacity, with 9,754 uniformed personnel out of an authorized 12,640 deployed as of March 2015. The UN is "stretched" and France has reduced its forces from four thousand during peak fighting in 2013 to three thousand spread across five countries in the Sahel, with a growing focus on Boko Haram, according to IHS Jane. While AQIM is no longer dominant in Mali, continued instability in the country has allowed the group to retrench and expand in some areas.

The U.S. State Department says "the best strategy for dealing with AQIM remains working with regional governments to increase their capability, foster regional cooperation, and counter violent extremism." While Algiers has abjured a direct counterterrorism role for Western powers—namely, the United States and France—it has welcomed indirect support, according to CRS.

The George W. Bush administration established the Trans-Sahara Counterterrorism Partnership in 2005 to "take a holistic approach to countering violent extremism," providing civilian and military assistance to more than half a dozen partner countries in the Maghreb and Sahel—$44.3 million in fiscal year 2013. However, the U.S. Government Accountability Office found that TSCP lacked a strategy beyond bilateral aid and has faced challenges from the outset. Mali is the third partner country since 2008 to experience a military coup, after Mauritania and Niger, which triggers a suspension of security assistance under U.S. la

Al Murabitun

At the end of August 2013, the Katibat al-Muslimeen (Veiled Brigade) of Mokhtar Belmokhtar, announced a merger with the Movement for Unity and Jihad in West Africa (MUJWA) to create a new jihadist movement, al-Murabitun (The Almoravids). According to its founding statement, the group aims at pursuing the unity of all the Jihadist groups "from the Nile to the Atlantic". The group also stressed its allegiance to al-Qaeda and the Taliban by greeting "the leaders of jihad in this time," al-Qaeda leader Dr. Ayman al-Zawahiri and Afghan Taliban leader Mullah Omar.

France, responsible for expelling the jihadists from Mali earlier this year, was singled out in the statement, which called for jihadists to attack French interests "wherever they may be found." The group also described the Muslim Brotherhood's ouster from power in Egypt as proof of the assault of secular forces against Islam. However, the identity of the group's new Amir remains unclear, with Belmokhtar announcing his intention of forgoing leadership of the group to allow a new generation of jihadist leaders to come to the fore.

From an operational point of view, al-Murabitun may be considered a regional competitor to al-Qaeda in the Islamic Maghreb (AQIM). While the two groups will continue to have the same strategic aim—imposing Shari'a in the region—their short-term aims as well as tactics and strategies are different.

Belmokthar's relations with AQIM leadership remain particularly tense. The appointment of Jamal Oukacha (a.k.a. Yahya Abu al-Hammam)—a close ally of AQIM leader Abd al-Malik Droukdel-—as AQIM's Saharan Amir was an attempt by AQIM's central leadership to regain control over Belmokhtar and the movement's Sahelian battalions. At the same time, the spectacular actions of Belmokhtar—such as the In Aménas attack in Algeria in January and the May attacks in Niger—are considered more harmful than helpful in the eyes of AQIM.

Such attacks may push external actors to increase pressure on the group, which, after the defeat in Mali and the loss of several organizational leaders (most notably Abu Zeid), is more interested in reorganizing its ranks and operational networks. The fact that the leader of this new group is apparently not Algerian and the presence of MUJWA fighters in its ranks suggest that this is the final stage of a process started several years ago: the ethno-national pluralization of northern African jihad activities.

While AQIM continues to remain an Algerian-led and Algerian-focused organization, jihadists from Mauritania, Mali, the Western Sahara, Niger, southern Libya and Chad now represent an important reality on the ground and the birth of al-Murabitun reflects this change. The focus is becoming more regional, as was made clear by the historical references provided by MUJWA when it split from AQIM .

A second element of differentiation is the focus of Belmokhtar on immediate actions, while AQIM leader Abd al-Malik Droukdel has stressed over the last two years the need to act gradually in order to avoid powerful external pressures and friction with local Muslim communities. Despite these differences, it is still likely that members from the two organizations will cooperate at some point, as the organizational boundaries between all the groups operating in Northern Africa are rather thin and the same members—above all, low-ranking militants—may fight and operate under different labels and affiliations according to the circumstances.

The birth of al-Murabitun adds a new brand to the already dense and fragmented environment of Northern Africa jihadism. The name of the new group recalls a series of specific features of northern Africa's history under the reign of the Almoravids, especially the search for Muslim unity, Islamic purity and the fight against external enemies.

Although Belmokhtar has taken a step back by renouncing the leadership of this brand new group, his choice confirms his importance in the overall balance of North African jihadism, a particularly remarkable result for a person believed dead in March-April 2013. The Murabitun, despite having the same strategic aims as AQIM, will compete with the elder organization to some degree for a variety of reasons, primarily the personal friction between Belmokhtar and Droukdel. However, tactical and short-term convergences are more than likely on specific aims and operations, and the boundaries between these organizations will remain porous and often indistinguishable.

Jund al Khilafa

Jund al-Khilafah was previously a faction of al-Qaeda in the Islamic Maghreb, the Al Qaeda affiliate in North and West Africa. AQIM grew out of Algerian Islamist groups that had fought in the 1990s Civil War. Abdelmalek Gouri (who would later lead Jund al-Khilafah) was formerly the "right-hand man" of Abdelmalek Droukdel, who was the leader of AQIM. Gouri was also part of an AQIM cell responsible for suicide attacks on the government's headquarters and the UN compound in Algiers in 2007. He was also behind an attack in Iboudrarene in April 2014 that left 11 Algerian soldiers dead.

On 14 September 2014, the leader of al-Qaeda in the Islamic Maghreb (AQIM) in the central region, Khaled Abu Suleiman (nom de guerre of Abdelmalek Gouri), announced in a communique he was breaking allegiance with al-Qaeda and took an oath of allegiance to the leader of Islamic State of Iraq and the Levant, Abu Bakr al-Baghdadi. He was reportedly joined by an AQIM commander of an eastern region of Algeria. He claimed that other members of AQIM had "deviated from the right path" and declared to al-Baghdadi "*You have in the Islamic Maghreb men who will obey your orders.*"

A new armed group calling itself the "Soldiers of the Caliphate in Algeria" has split from al-Qaeda's North African branch and sworn loyalty to the group calling itself the Islamic State (IS), fighting in Syria and Iraq. In a communique released, a regional commander of al-Qaeda in the Islamic Maghreb (AQIM) said he broke away from the group, accusing it of "deviating from the true path".

Gouri Abdelmalek, nom de guerre Khaled Abu Suleimane, claimed leadership of the splinter group, and was joined by a AQIM commander of an eastern region in Algeria. The "Soldiers of the Caliphate in Algeria" is the latest group to break with AQIM and side with Baghdadi, after veteran Algerian jihadist, Mokhtar Belmokhtar's group, "Those who sign in Blood" pledged allegiance to the IS group.

But experts say the announcement will not have a major operational impact on the ground as AQIM has been focused on the Sahel region rather than OPEC member Algeria.

Jund al Khilafa, or "Soldiers of the Caliphate," claimed responsibility for the beheading of French tourist Herve Gourdel last year. Since the beheading, the group has reportedly suffered severe setbacks from the Algerian military. Late last year, the government said that it killed the leader of Jund al Khilafa and several other members of the group. In May, more than 20 members were killed in an ambush in Bouira province. The new emir of the Islamic State branch in Algeria was killed in that ambush.

The report of Abdelmalek's death comes roughly three months after Jund al Khilafa -- a small Islamist group formerly linked to al Qaeda -- published a video showing the beheading of Gourdel in what the group said was a display of support to al Qaeda's rival ISIS.

Gourdel, 55, was hiking in central Algeria's Djudjura National Park when he was abducted in September. Jund al Khilafa, having just declared allegiance to the Islamic State in Iraq and Syria (ISIS), then published a video of Gourdel's beheading on September 24.

The video was titled, "A message of blood for the French government." The group said it was responding to an appeal by ISIS spokesman Muhammad al-Adnani to kill "the spiteful and filthy French" because of their support for military action against the group in Iraq.

A video message showing the execution was designed to resemble beheadings carried out by ISIS, as were the words of one of the militants, who said: "*Let the French people know that their blood is cheap for their President, and it is the same as you made the blood of the Muslim women and children cheap in Iraq and Sham (Syria)."*

The Algerian government called the beheading an act of "criminals," and French President Francois Hollande said at the time that Algeria's Prime Minister assured him he would do the utmost to find the killers. Algerian army launched its attack in Isser after tracking what it believed was "a dangerous terrorist group driving a vehicle" in the city, the Algerian defense ministry said. Abdelmalek was later confirmed as one of the three that the army killed.

Gourdel was just one of the Westerners to be beheaded by an Islamist extremist group this year. Since mid-August, ISIS has beheaded American journalists Steven Sotloff and James Foley, British aid worker David Haines, British aid convoy volunteer Alan Henning, and American aid worker Peter Kassig.

Ansar Dine

Ansar Dine is a paramilitary terrorist group of insurgents based in Northern Mali but operating throughout the country to impose Sharia law. Their primary operations are against the Mali military and opposing rebel groups. In 2012 they captured the caravan town of Timbuktu and imposed strict Islamic law on a previously moderate and tolerant society. In the global war on terrorism, they are associated with the Islamic groups AQLIM, National Movement for the Liberation of Azawad (MNLA), al Qaeda in the Lands of the Islamic Maghreb (AQIM), and the Tuareg Rebels.

Background

Iyad Ag Ghali is a 54 years old Malian. He is the leader of Ansar Dine. From the region of Kidal, northern Mali, Iyad Ag Ghali is a Irayakan, family of the Ifoghas. It is in Libya, however, where he made his debut in the early 1980s: in his early twenties he chose to join the Islamic Legion of Colonel Gaddafi

In Libya, Ag Ghali manages to get noticed. He was sent to Lebanon to fight the phalanges and Christians, according to some sources, aside from some shooting in Chad, in the course of the 1980s, before returning to Mali when the "Guide" declares the dissolution of the Legion.

Ag Ghali is disappointed, but soon found another cause to champion, becoming one of the leading figures of the Tuareg rebellion: it was he who, at the head of the Popular Movement for the Liberation of Azawad (MPLA), attacked the town of Menaka, June 28, 1990. Six months later, the Tamanrasset agreements were signed under the auspices of Algeria, brought an end to the fighting, but the rebels were deeply divided.

Ag Ghali founded the Popular Movement of Azawad (MPA), which brought together the most moderate Tuaregs, he didn't hesitate to confront his former companions and sometimes to allied with the Malian army... His military superiority isn't doubted. For many Malians he is the one that brought peace to the North in the late 1990s.

Gradually, the man got in to contact with radical preachers like the Pakistani Jamaat al-Tabligh ("association for preaching"). In 1999 Iyad Ag Ghali has changed: he stopped shaking hands with women, made his wife wear a veil and spends most of his free time in mosques. Surprising? Not so much. This radicalization is associated with a strong anti-Western sentiment, sharpened in training camps in Libya. In addition, the economic crisis has pushed many Malians, both sedentary and nomadic, into the arms of religion.

In 2003, Ag Ghali is involved with the fundamentalist cause, but not Jihadism: he said to be hostile to terrorism and suicide bombings. This "state of mind" makes him the ideal intermediary to negotiate the release of hostages held by Islamic Salafist Group for Preaching and Combat (GSPC). Thus, in August of the same year the government in Bamako asked Ag Ghali to intercede with Abou Zeid for European tourists kidnapped in Algeria – which he did with success.

Three years later, in May 2006, the anger is brewing again in Northern Mali. Tuareg accuse the authorities of failing to meet their commitments. Ag Ghali meets with President Amadou Toumani Toure (ATT), but negotiations fall short. He then approaches Ibrahim Ag Bahanga, another great figure from irredentist Tuareg, who died in August 2011. Algeria is again involved, obtains the signature of new agreements for peace (the Algiers Accords, signed in July 2006) and, as in the previous uprising, Ag Ghali traded his fighting uniform for a uniform of a man of peace.

Ahmada Ag Bibi

Ahmada Ag Bibi and Iyad Ag Ghali know each other for a long time. In the early 1990s already, they both were in the People's Movement of Azawad (MPA). Ag Bibi is a great activist for the Tuareg cause, but that does not stop to soak in more obscure cases and to be linked to negotiations for the release of Western hostages. In Ag Bibi's address book there are bandits, smugglers, politicians in Bamako and Algiers, and even members of several intelligence services (he was a member of the parliamentary committee Defense and Homeland Security). Also he was the chairman of the parliamentary group for Mali-Algeria friendship and in November 2011 he accompanied the former colonel in the French army, Jean-Marc Gadoullet, to negotiate for the release of Abu Zayd AREVA and VINCI hostages.

When the North rose again in January 2012, Ag Bibi joined the MNLA and Ansar Dine, driven by both realism and friendship towards Ag Ghali. He is not attached to secularism, but believes, as the Ansar Dine diplomat Alghabass Ag Intallah, in negotiating "peaceful solutions" and could therefore be the man to talk to. "Only Algeria can play a role of mediator between the parties to the conflict," he said.

Ag Mohamed Najim, another veteran of the Islamic Legion who Ag Ghali cordially detests, is therefore preferred. This is a slap for Ag Ghali but he didn't mind. He created his own training group, Ansar Dine. Probably he hoped to cause dislocation of MNLA, which weaknesses he knows so well the. At the same time, Ag Ghali also renounced to become the successor of the amenokal (traditional leader) of Ifoghas, the old Intallah Ag Attaher preffered his son, Alghabass Intallah Ag. Again, the bitterness is strong, but he cannot afford to openly confront the patriarch.

It is better to deal and work hand in hand with Ag Intallah, who is highly respected in the region. Ag Ghali holds his hand in June 2012. The MNLA is dying, and now it is Ansar Dine which discuss with the mediator of the Economic Community of West Africa (ECOWAS), President Blaise Compaoré of Burkina Faso. The former soldier of Gaddafi is now recognized as a key player in the Malian crisis. If he distanced himself from the Salafists, as incited by foreign diplomats, he might even become an ally. Moreover, if he considers that direct confrontation with AQIM can serve his ambitions, he will not hesitate to turn against its current "partners". Abou Zeid, Mokhtar Ould Mohamed Hamada and Belmokhtar Kheirou know better than anyone else.

Alghabass Ag Intallah

Originally Alghabass Ag Intallah isn't a warlord. As a member of the National Assembly, he is especially the son of the powerful Ifoghas chief and his designated successor – a line that allows him to benefit from many contacts into the Persian Gulf, including the royal family of Qatar. When the Tuareg rebellion broke out in January 2012, he first ranked alongside the National Movement for the Liberation of Azawad (MNLA) – though always advocated for dialogue with Bamako – then rallied Ansar Dine. Ag Intallah is not a fanatic, and his choice is probably more pragmatic – the fragmentation of MNLA is unequivocal – ideologically. Today, Ag Intallah is the political face of Ansar Dine, it's ambassador. He is the one who is received by the mediator of the crisis, the Burkinabe President Blaise Compaore. Iyad Ag Ghali knows too much for having interest in linking his fate to reign Ifoghas.